Whispers from The Multiverse

Poems from The AfroDeep

by Regina YC Garcia

Whispers from The Multiverse: Poems from the AfroDeep

Cover art: Regina YC Garcia

ISBN 978-0-9852877-3-3

Willow Books, a Division of Aquarius Press

www.WillowLit.net

Printed in the United States of America

Dedication

On Earth...

This book is dedicated to my most beloveds on earth—Romeo Garcia, Jr and the three who formed in and beneath my heart—Romeo, III, Rafael, and Royan.

In the Heavens...

This work of my heart is written in memory of those whose voices still whisper from the skies—*Evelyn, Bessie, Nettie, Reba, Carrie, Margaret, Cinda, and on and on....*

Contents

*Indicates previously published

Afrofutures Revelation Multiverse–**Black is a well**

A sense of rightness, a sense of self. It was nothing when you had it. You hardly noticed. But once it was missing, it was like a sliver of fruit on a long sea voyage, the difference between bleeding gums and survival.

—Chibundu Onuzo from *Sankofa*

Black is a well

Deep
That is
what must be
said, deep and dark
dark, deep like a well
Like a well, stretched bottom unending

Unending
That is
what must be
said, unending and full
full, unending like invisible tears
Like invisible tears, bitter and sweet

Sweet
That is
what must be
said, sweet like knowing

knowing, sweet like whispered promise
Like whispered promise, like oracles, prophecy

Prophecy
That is
what must be
said, prophecy like hope
hope, quietly prophesying, being sentient
Like sentient histories, dead and living

Living
That is
what must be
said, living and creating
creating living from no way
Like sending way buckets into blackness

Blackness
That is
what must be
said, Blackness and lifting
lifting eyes towards dark skies
Like skyways, folkways, Diaspora, *Sankofa*

Sankofa
That is
what must be
said, *Sankofa*, remembering, gathering
gathering for today and tomorrow
Like tomorrow is *well*...beautiful...*Black*

Black
is a
well, welling
in my soul…

High John (Ipomoea Jalapa, Bindeweed, Jalop Root)

"Like King Arthur of England, he has served his people. And, like King Arthur, he is not dead. He waits to return when his people shall call him again … High John de Conquer went back to Africa, but he left his power here, and placed his American dwelling in the root of a certain plant. Only possess that root, and he can be summoned at any time."

Zora Neale Hurston in "High John De Conquer"

High John manifests
running wild in fields
crouching low in gardens
even burrowing underground
heeding whispers and chants
for more, for better, ignoring
those who doubt his power
to restore health, to improve
conditions, to bear the fortune, to find courage
He has followed those stolen, those sorrowed,
those steadily holding hope that he will find
them, and his power will transcend their trouble

Over here, High John

High John, so high
the Saints still call him
The Orishas cry out, rumble 'round
to find him, to guide him, to reveal
him, he, unassuming, lowly, powerful and

holy, he moves through, from tall grass to clearing
and arrives holding fortune in one hand and
healing in the other, pours assurance from his
mouth and illuminates love to the seeking
and the scorned from lips dripping in honey and humility

Oh, High John

High John comes
He could've stayed away
but he could not leave his
people, as they entreated, danced
in clearings stump drums thumping the night

Yea, High John

High John arrives
Golden straw crown gleaming
Making ways for his people who
have wailed, wandered, waited, watched
fatigued and faltering...He still sees the holes to fill
that they might somehow become whole, as whole as he who has scoured
the lands and the seas

Draw near, High John

High John finds and fixes
and pulls from robes a

Conqueror's Cure

God is within her, she will not fall; God will help her at break of day.

Psalms 46:5 NIV

At Daybreak

Everybody is clutching and grabbing
trying to hold on to the fragments of love
sparsely scattered throughout a day
She is searching for *hers*
in between the protruding glass, while
the air witnesses and threatens that tearfalls will
cause her to stumble face first into the shards
piercing her eyes…her heart
Yet, she still walks, half knowing of the words and
presence of the wise women with and before her

and the god that has kept *them*
They murmur and then remind from above and around…,

God is within her; she will not fall

It is again the break of day, and trouble is still *troubling*
Circles of sin, putting on grins and enticing
her to leave what she *knows* her mothers believed–
that in *her* is a spirit known well to *woe*, and no ordinary

man could've…would've told her that his hands would be so hot
and his heart, so cold…
This story, so old that it whirls in like
a possessed harbinger screeching
within the fellowship of memories, breaking the peace…

They say to her, "don't count on your own mind…it has been
tainted with an unreasonable hope… tie yourself to sense"

…and more they *say,* and then they *sing* and *pray*
and she, not afraid enough, walks her own way while the mothers
move unseen around and behind, holding their peace
breath having been long gone

One says to the others something about *time*
and one of the others says back "Give it to her"
God is within her; She will not fall…
as they wait with an old woman's hope
for the breaking of the next day

Waterproofed

You sang.

Walk togedder, chillen,

Dontcha git weary. . . .

The strong men keep a-comin' on

The strong men git stronger.

–Sterling Brown from "Strong Men"

My Mama was insistent–she wanted her children to swim–something about her not "learning how" in her youth.

Maybe the "not learning" had something to do with little access, little brown children not being allowed in pools, public or private, in the Jim Crow South, where and when she grew up, or

maybe it had something to do with having to accomplish what had to be done to carve out a life worth living for herself and her family, or

maybe, just maybe, there was a fear etched into collective memory, a lingering fear that the water often took in but did not always bear up live bodies…

those original memories having been collected upon the sorrowful witness of our enslaved ancestral kinsman, trafficked

on boats, so distraught by the horrors already begun and the others sure to come, that they leapt from the ships into the sea.

Whatever the reason, she determined that we would be "waterproofed," my sisters and I. She even took lessons herself in adulthood although she claimed there was a critical period for learning how to do it well.

So, we swam, summer after summer, even participating in the Parks and Rec swim team, and when we left the fold, married and had children, she insisted on paying for their lessons and would attend those lessons whenever she could…

Mama declared that it was one of the most important skills to have, and while I wondered about the obsession, I never questioned it. I loved the water, but for her, being able to conquer any fears and not be pulled under was vital.

I thought about this yesterday, as I witnessed a young brother in Montgomery, Alabama leap into the murky river water, swim towards the fray, focus on the danger, and not be consumed…a beautiful movement of love to help his people…

My mother marched in The Movement…

In her lifetime, Mama listened to and breathed the winds of change, crossed broken earth, spoke fire, and equipped her charges to glide through water…

a necessary movement…

Yesterday, something…moved in me…moved in others…

Keep moving…

MotherGod

Eve knows of woe
Black, Blamed, Betrayed…
Moving & migrating, her restless seeds
have blown into the wind- some landing close, some
spreading into the far reaches- shifting yet evolving- changing
skin, hair, face- losing memory…

Misdirected

Her children have oft rejected her
Reviled the magic of her birth cries, loss
cries, the knowledge of her existence, her sonar screams
So, she has searched silently, wrapped in woe, collecting some
of their pieces from ocean floors, whispering into the blocked ears
built by burned histories, lost divinity…They live consumed by material
power… Oblivious to her watch…

Blinded

She wants nothing from them but for them
to live, to fly, to love themselves, each other

…before it's too late

...be like–a rumination

what will this world be like when we can no longer hear the song of the refugee, when all the doors are shut hard & babies with razored teeth stand beside the decaying bodies, alone & remembering, hungry & ever shifting these thoughts about the goodness of man, the purpose of piety, the futility of dreams &

what will this world be like when skin & tissue & bone become properties owned by fear & flesh who fight with fake affront, commandeering pulp, sanctioning love, enslaving rinds &

what will this world be like when the sun affixes itself low & brooding & scorches the evil & those less so & those who silently watched, melting without a word, emotion dried beyond tears &

what will it be like when the buildings & altars collapse & crumble &

the gods move on...

Anansi Unbroken

Anansi
slid himself under shackles
between wrought iron and ankles, for
despite his play, he understood that this was no joke, and no counsel in darkness
would indeed, hearken the darkest end

Anansi
so, he traveled with them, furling and unfurling hairy tendrils, reaching,
weaving plans in the corner of minds…stitching lips closed…deftly
plucking threads out…

as Time whispered to him
Tell them when to speak and when not

when to bear, when to run, when to hide
when to fight, when to
push pride into another space in their minds
how to live to see another day, how to say goodbye, how to spin webs of protection
for those sold away…

…how to construct families of those from other nations bound to the brutality of the new lands

whether dry sand
whether barren soil
whether accursed clay
whether frozen block
whether wet hot hellish earth…

Anansi

created trickster, friend of fickle and folly found his highest calling

while whispering words of survival

Often times feet up
Often times heads down
Smiles covered
yet they smiled
Laughter concealed
yet they laughed
Plan subversive
yet they planned
Ghost immersive
yet they lived

Anansi

Master of shade and creator of shadings
Seamed curtains around clearings
as The Skin tethered to misery
communed with the God
of all gods, differently named by diverse tongues…

Yea, this Great Spirit fell like cooling water in raging fires, upon them raining shrouds of hope…

My, how they danced…my, how they prayed… my, how they praised…

…in this broken unknown land!

Anansi

Diasporic traveler of many names and forms who still lives in mouths and subconscious memories of his people for…

…those who still cry out
…those who still seek
…those who want to know the stories

Washed All Over

Mami Wata/stirred the seas/& pulled up from the murky bottoms/ truth & stolen memory/ In anger/ my auntie spawned a tsunami with a single flip of her mighty tail/& as it rolled up & towards the shore/ The Wave reminded The Air to scorch & thin the space/between those- The Unrepentant & The Highest God/ that the infidels might finally hear & bow down to The Truth that could wash over them/ that could save them/ at last

Beat Drops

From war darkened skies/ winged bronzed & blackened women/ dive into and in between the fray/ Their ancient weapons of war forged in boat bottoms/ from torn skin/fingernails/ metal shavings of shackles/formed invisible/ dedicated on high spiritual altars/ polished & anointed with blood & tears/and inserted as an impenetrable sword replacing spine/ Bone essence from the waters gild ribs as gold/ that wings might pull in/ out/ In those times as in these/these wings invisible to purposed predators/ emerge large/adorned/ to lift up the guardians/War sounds surround death camps/ heralding their entrance like ancient drum beats dropping/ heavy whooshing & flapping/ in an urgent new day

Afrofutures Haiku in Multiverse-Brown Girl Surfs the Continuum

Scanning the timeline
Brown girl roaming, mind in flight
Be vigilant, now!

"Lives depend on hope
Consult every star you find"
Croons Mother of Days

She crossed deep oceans
Found emerging life forms
Clay shaped with divine breath

Life struggled with sin
Centers distended, bore life
Learned more, grew smart, strong

Below this star bright
Sparkling clean waters quenched earth
Love and fear bloomed sure

sacrificed shine

moonman has gone under the sea[1]
following the path of darkness-light-into
the depths

this is not impossible to believe
for the absence of celestial-born atmosphere
will not disrupt his ability to descend

maybe soon silvery fins will grow
and sustaining gills will emerge

maybe he will shed his moonman name

maybe soon

for the lonely
now-moonless sky
is far away

and maybe what dwells beneath
will love him and allow him stay

---

1 from Christopher Okigbo, "Transition" https://hursandryder.wordpress.com/2019/09/25/transition/

praying
for him/for *them*
because I know in my heart that
moonman has always loved
moody sea

this is why he rocks her back and forth
every evening time, giving her space
to empty and refill

in/out back/forth

always beautifying her from above
with his cherished moonlight spill

alas, problematic proximity
may coax him back from under sea
and post himself high as he spies
his beloved's frantic despair

for she soon-saddened sea
can no longer anticipate
her lover's life-giving moonlight stare

Maybe God is The Moon

Maybe it was the Moon
that bore me up
placed me on its Moon back
when my light was low
so low I could not speak,
could not utter, when I was
sliced and excluded from
my own voice

Maybe it was the Moon that
circled me through stages,
plunged me into cold and
silent darkness, turned me away
from the light of a prideful sun,
shocked and awakened my skin,
nestled me in craters where my
breath did not matter, allowed me to
emerge in stages so that I,
perched high, could witness that
indeed, the wages of living is Death,
paid early or late, and the tides
will live longer than I

Maybe it was the Moon that tenderly
slid me down its beam back into the fray
reminded me of how to walk, to hide, to emerge
to cry for, to try to find a
human space of other *MoonMadeOvers*

Maybe it was the Moon that reanimated
my soul, filled it with purpose, taught me
how to line this pathway back to wherever
I need to be….

Blue

The color blue indicates a temperature even hotter than white. Blue flames usually appear at a temperature between 2,600° F and 3,000° F

—from "Greensickness" by Laurel Chen

The poet said…

She said—*Grief is not the only geography I know*

& my heart thumped loudly in affirmation & sorrow & fear

for I can plot clouds that hang dark & black & and low

whose water cannot quench

the blue flames of this fire

bluest despair, bluest depravity

driven by derision & exclusion & death…

The bluest eye scorches outward & deep to find

the flaw in poverty & pain &

it glories as it sees no

promise running wild across a loveless terrain…

This bluest burning orb rotates inward to its god

and offers sacrifice

I know well the land charted as chasms ever-widening

swallowing dreams

I know well the land blackened-blue from the unchecked flaming of
self-anointed authority

For in this land, the brilliance of sky & the cool of sea
have no say
& layers peel away
incinerated into nothingness
as we burn inside-outside-in
embodied in horror

This is the land on which I live
I am brought here to stand atop
to add to the mounting mourning of
ashes & darkened weary bones

Speculation

If our forebears could've

'died their torture' (just once)

& buried the institution of depravity

(just once)

& burned the *humiliation* of that which

happened

& spread the ashes deeply in dark soil

& placed a guard over it

& sealed it in silence

& reverence

& put the pain to bed (just once)

Perhaps this collective trauma, this *remembrance of shame,* would not have

awakened in the generations showering

the wounding whispers that madly

echo the lie (over & over again)

the captors' lie (over & over again)

uncivilized (over & over)

uncultured (over & over)

inhuman (over & over)

you children of nowhere-no language, no land, no history (over & over)

If we could have just kept these
murderous words
from seeping into our bones
& passing through our life seed
& filtering into muddled minds
& settling into ulcerated places
& casting them onto others

Perhaps, *if we could've killed it…*
(just once)

five midnight men clothed in
protectors' blue
badge-pinned shimmering
brown skin gleaming in the glare of
street lights/headlights/sky cams
would've chosen peace over pummeling

& perhaps

Suspected recklessness would have been verified or put to rest with no notions of
bashing batons

taser's shock

flights of fists

compounding kicks

& perhaps

those wrapped in enforcement

authority

could have understood

the true toll of the terror

of disappearing flesh

of stifled breath

inflicted in the then

in the now

...when humanizing peace does not abide

& perhaps...

if they had known it

if we had known it/killed it

Tyre Nichols

could have gotten up

three days later…

with all power in his hands

instead of being one more

black boy

gushing blood red

100 yards from his house

piteously wailing for his mama

Over and over again

Harriet: Blood and Bones

My bones, not my bones
My blood, not my blood
My life, not my life
As you have seen fit to lift me &
carry me over trees & through
darkness & dankness go I
Shrouded and moving from one way
station to the next & I would be
no mother to even one

He insists, opening my enslaved
womb & filling it with divine
purpose, depositing
the holiest spirit
to reside & contract & push out a
new manifestation
a handmaiden of
Freedom.

Propel me forward
Wrench me back
Innumerable times have you
spangled stars that
I might see *Me*

Against

Everything

Birthing

Freedom

Finding My Way…

I jest about not being a "flower writer"
See, my heart has a hard time finding them-
flowers—
in my writing

But today the poet said (reminded my heart)
that the healing lies in nature
& if I could but pluck & place my hurt
in its field then
maybe I could find the restoration
that my old mothers and I desperately seek

I call the flora and fauna
that I might bask & renew under sky
…above ground

I lay rocks along the dark path
where day flowers oddly awaken &
stand as sentinels along these trails
down which so many were dragged
struggling/screaming

They give you the ceremony/the language
These old ones do
These ancestors do

Black Blues Gone

Pulled from collective memory

On cold mornings
My grandmother would light the stove with
fire and dry kindling to warm the house and
our stomachs. She would heat sweet potatoes
still in their rough papery skin from the night before
One day I rose, earlier than usual, & saw her walking
outside of my brown bag-sealed window
tattered coat collar pulled around her ears, woolen socks
pulled over her hands & as she bent and reached towards the woodpile
I saw the grimace & wince replace the
soft brown gentleness of her face. This was the first time
I had seen her as anything
but God

Poor & black we were, but she never allowed us to feel
the sting of the pain of this existence
nor experience the skewed culture often birthed from
abject poverty & exclusion
She was our Savior, & we resided in her courts
covered by her care until such time
as our skin toughened to the world

Her garden bloomed as if
it knew her & loved her

her touch, her talk, her tenderness
It lifted up offerings of
fresh vegetables, enough for her to can for long winter months
& sprouted lush herbs for healing balms
She fed and treated all she knew who needed her care
She fought through pain to create a path for promise
The blue of Blackness in this cruel south would not
deter her resolve to tend her people
in her garden of hope

Some of us are rivers…

Though they may be beautiful
flooding and fascinating their beds
You can't always trust the rivers
They are moon mad mavens of mystery
Sometimes rushing rapids
Sometimes flat serenity

You cannot always trust the rivers
Spilling over banks
Raising praise hands
towards the fickle shine

You can't always trust the rivers
The spirits that inhabit them
fight to direct their flow

Yet, she will have…
they will have…
the very last say

" This was his home. But now he would have to leave, for the water was rising and there was no telling when or where it would stop"

-Richard Wright

Uncle Tom's Children, 1938

River Tears

I. ...even The River

& The Voice cried

Let there be...

& it was so

& it was all so...

so loved

All Creation

was loved

even The River

Creature House

Watered Way

Holder of the newest secrets of
a blooming & budding earth

flowing to & through

a seeing & knowing
Witness of Love

until…

II. The River Waits

This old dry bed waits for the rain to move ancient sediment downstream

its hot mouth exposed & yearning

It waits for new life to fall from the sky like it once did-

raging & flooding
overflowing its banks
taking in the forlorn living
spitting out the bloated dead

polishing captured stones & bones

trapping dark secrets

keeping confidences

covering truths

feeding ravenous spirits

drenching the professed redeemed…

sanctifying *them*

This old dry bed will open wide its rough gravely mouth for water like wine

gurgle greedily & anger in the *not-enough*-ness

determine that if it ever fills again, it will take back all that it has lost

as soon as what was lost wanders within its reach-

the young & the old

the prepared & the unready

the holy & the wicked…

I will not be fooled

I have not forgotten

There will be righteous fury

There will be…

    Revolution

III. **Black Forth Back**

Is this gift too late?
It, turning up after I'm dead
    …after we are all dead
The pushing, the pulling, the running
the breath, the beating, the dying…
    Is it too late?
The river has seen it all &
angry, it has run in its righteousness
polluted with exsanguinated corpses
    & dreams
It ebbs in tire
tides rocking in & out
    in and out
from age to age
Yet, these ancient incantations persist
in the mouths of elders & their ghosts
chants that float back time
& bring the Long Dead
    the Too Late
back to living
back to loving
worthy of love

delivered to love

Whole

I knew/We knew the victim before the story broke…

Let me be clear-She is not the murder nor the murderer.

She is *The Murdered.*

She was the opposite of what murder is, what murder does. She did not puncture nor torch nor tear down nor shoot nor oppress nor drain herself

I say this because…

we currently have no name for the assailant/assailants

& sometimes Our Dead are tried for dying

79 years old

She lived, was living, helped others live…

She still lives in our mouths, in our memories, in our hearts

Currently, she floats with ancestors & the angels

Even though, before the story broke, her family was calling for her, wondering where, reaching out…

"Where is she?"

They surely said this, over & over

I didn't hear it said, personally

but my heart knows that it was because I know them & I know her…*knew her…*

Before the story broke, a friend called me to tell me what was going on, that she had been found…

"…didn't seem like natural causes"

My friend heard…

…word whipping 'round early, soon as…*before the story broke*

& when the story broke, Greenville breathed in…blew out…stunned

I know…I was there…we were all there beside our Christmas trees

at our parties

next to the beds of loved ones who may have been living & struggling through their natural lives…anticipating natural causes

& we reached out to each other with phones & dipped fingers into virtual portals…

…posted the news, shared the story

Why…how…who would?

Lord have mercy…Have mercy Lord!

For the first time ever, I was glad my mother couldn't process this

her mind & memory not allowing the torturous revelation…

& now in the days that follow this story, building on my timeline post & in my ear pressed to receivers, I hear the intimate revelations of those stunned when the story broke

words of hurt, incredulity…

“Oh my God, my dear friend”

“I knew her well. She was a true leader”

“I knew her and her brother. They grew up with my Mom. So sad”

“Oh my God, this is horrible! She hired me years ago”

“She was my French teacher”

“My mother loved her and she would visit her when she came home”

“Such a sweet lady! She had a beautiful soul. My prayers are with the family. May she rest in peace…”

“She was such a sweet woman. This is so heartbreaking and sad. She didn't deserve this.”

& on and on, these words

of anger

of condolence

of disbelief

of grief

& even fear

I saw her last at a community poetry reading…she was my mama's best childhood and college friend…she always encourages me…

encouraged me…

& since that day, in these days

we "Happy" the New Year

& wait for word

& speculate

& pray for a person of interest to emerge

so that we might blow out all of our hurt

& anger

& fear towards this evil

this plague

that has broken

the broken flesh of

a dear & revered mother

of our culture

& despite our best efforts

not to…

For God knows what we don't…

&

We'll understand it better by and by…

…we ponder & grieve
the life of a person
whose human form was
in such close proximity to us
& murder
& so eerily reminiscent of
our own

She was…*is*…our own.

Elijah…*Surely*

In memory of the late Elijah McClain

February 25, 1996 – August 30, 2019

A few of his last known words:

You are beautiful. And I love you. Try to forgive me. I'm sorry.

Surely the air saw the young man walking
perhaps whispering to himself
& thinking, maybe, of the kittens he loved so
& the violin that calmed them and him and allowed
soothing expression-bow, string, bridge, wood, synchronized
filling night air, evoking smiles, belying the reality
of his peculiar, beautiful, diversity of learning and being…
I imagine, he made some onlookers smile, & they thought of him
as peace in the world, of love, a beloved, precocious, curious fellow
with a childlike tenderness, a sensitive soul…Just *surely*
he is missed as evidenced by the orchestra of the aggrieved who
swallowed their pain and poured it into the song that floated
into air, beyond clouds, and into the stars to which he *surely*, probably
no doubt escaped & curled in craters cushioned by creatures beloved
living their tenth life & soothed by drifting earthborn symphonic lullabies
ever-crooning, reminding him that he did
nothing wrong…
Surely, he was loved, by his mother, by others…
Surely

Lest It Be Built…

Powerful and terrified men have tried to carve structures of inclusion from the

mush of degradation

Scooped the soggy remnants from the rains of deadly days

Days that lacked humanity, even less equality

Fragile facades litter this land

Representing faux bastions of change

While racism, disparities, and brutality pour through systems

Molded by hands that move quickly and creep slowly for their own desired ends

Refusing to care that in the process of building, layering weakened bricks with the mortar of fear and privilege results in inevitable impermanence and massive destruction

We are now asked to meet on trembling platforms to accept the contract

Approve repairs

Celebrate the patchwork on these tenements of horror
As we have in days gone by
Even now, dying earlier and faster
Imprisoned quicker and longer
Murdered hands up, backs turned, cries and breath broken and obstructed
Calling for our mothers
Looking for our children
We are even asked to forget who we are
Deny our roots of pain and gain, from where we have come, how we imagined and created what we could not access, how we climbed out and moved ahead

Now, we are told to hand back our voices

Take the deal!

The Slumlords of Liberty are depending on us!

Do not shake their hands.

Black Bodied

"In the 1840s, the Alabama physician James Marion Sims conducted infamous experimental gynecological surgery exclusively on black women, bound to the surgical table by chattel slavery, physical force and opium. The drug did not alleviate their pain, and some historians suggest that they became addicted to it."[2]

I. Black Then

*Lie Down/*Stretched and prodded/not even for her eventual ease/need/Every broken dream/Every broken body/ Expendable/*For white use only/*for sacrifice/ Hungry knives carved tender skin/ heat singed/the softest parts/ the previously violated/previously worked/previously whipped/previously forced to bear more/to turn the wheels/to increase their labor/Pleas disregarded/without favor/like Black/women/*others/* screaming/drugged into madness/ calling Death/surely/to save themselves/

back then

---

2 Harriet Washington, "Book and Arts," Nature, 26 February 2019,26 June 2024, https://www.nature.com/articles/d41586-019-00340-5#:~:text=In%20the%201840s%2C%20the%20Alabama,they%20became%20addicted%20to%20it.

II. Black Now

We need to operate/This baby/...too large/ .... will not fit/.... narrow

*heart-shaped pelvis/*My eyes/rooted around/for my husband's eyes/They

catch mine//gleam assurance/*They know what to do/* Nurse prepares
slender tube/

for insertion/*Will this hurt? / Will there be medication?* /No response/
Narrow catheter navigates

upward/ *into* the narrow space/that only ever knew the way *out/*I heard
my own moan cut the air/

*Relax/*Urethra angrily convulses response/at the betrayal/ Nurse contin-
ues/undaunted/ Preps for

next phase/The elusive pain medicine/finally emerges/*after.... /*

My *heart* felt/ the cost of/ *otherness/*

Even *then/*Even *now*

“My mother always falling”

from Reginald Shepherd, “No White Dove”

My mother was a tree, was a river

My mother was a tree, was a river

My mother stood tall; my mother ran down secrets; my mother dredged up truths

My mother walked towards Danger, slept with it, pulled out a knife, dared it to kill her

My mother was steadfast, moved quickly in resolve, moved silently to ensure

My mother was a reaper, scythe slicing what dared remove her/us

My mother was *Beauty*, wore wispy red curls,

and donned dresses

that hugged her petite brown frame

My mother was assassinated many times, and many times she rose again

My mother was full of trembling fullness that her face never revealed

My mother was brimming with a heat

that you might never know of before you felt the burn

My mama….

My mother–sometimes *falling* like a tree

My mother–never let it…us…*fall*

My mother–always rising righteous

My mother–lifting praise hands

My mother loving, living, dying

My mother–laughing like *she be knowing* Heaven is really real

The Body Grows Weapons…

My body grows weapons to protect my borders
It breeds tiny needles in my throat
& gleaming knives that
break out and into skin, over and again
to slash and bind the consequences
of the dark sins that threaten to rise
& live again
Border breach from within!
Stitch it down
Press it in
or stake it to the tree
to bleed out into
this parched earth

My body grows weapons to protect my borders
& seeks to keep me safe from the repercussions of
a world that wants to be *great again*
So, my tongue cocks & rapid fires to stop the shame again
of a country that would not have me remember
my history & removes
my martyred names
again

My body grows weapons to protect my borders

to stave off the hoarders that would strip all that I have
reach inside my brain & my throat
still my heart
tear my family apart
deny my beauty, deep and dark
steal my offerings
render my aspirations
unholy, untrue
Not for you
No woman like you
No woman like you
No woman like you

My body grows weapons to protect my borders
For fear sounds like
gun clicks
aimed at the flesh temples
of my beloved
lying on corners
in beds
in clubs
just for
Looking
Living
Loving
Desiring to be

a part of the *we*

who deserve protection

& I open my borders to those

who need

who covet

the concept of "Free to be..."

My body grows weapons to protect my borders

& all who dwell within

I pull all who dwell, within

I offer my unsilent mouth

to suck the venom

& neutralize

the danger

of a bound &

bloodied world

AfroFutures: Guess you best forget

"What is your name?"
"Where are you from?"

Guess you best forget

Nations of people
Broken
Lives bartered for the disposal of memory
Now, broken memory
Now, degraded dreams
All of this movement, dispossessing people
Of the knowledge of their culture
The glory of their past
The beauty of their movement
The victories they have won
The battles overcome
The richness of their land
Their reverence of life, of living, of death

This is a treacherous way to erase worlds

Still…

Guess you best forget

"Can't go back"

"Look ahead"

"Can't get off the boat"

"Keep walking"

"Slow down

"Stop"

Just forget

Pain replaces progress

Lynchings replace liberties

Shame replaces sight

Arrest replaces autonomy

Grief, ever present, from the

earliest days to this

Guess you best forget

Loss, however achieved, can make

People forget their names even

Beyond enslavement

Beyond imprisonment

Beyond swinging ropes

Beyond knees

Please…please

Beyond…

Guess you best forget

A life descended from a way of living
That snapped straightway the hopes
Of some of the strongest among those whose names were stolen away
Crushed by ropes, guns, systems

Silence

Tongues stilled
While bloodied mouths gurgled
Trying to call ancestors
Who ultimately materialize to carry them home
Calling their names as they fly
Dark bodies gleaming in the sky

Into the by and by

They want you to forget, but bay-bay…

On today
Some of these children out here are telling these stories
right now
They have found the ancient scrolls

They have talked to ancient souls

They see a future with

Contemporary processes and

Ancient magic, connected to an earth before

1492

1619

Plantations

Workhouses

Trails of tears

Tracks and dynamite

Internment camps

Torn up tenements

Can I get a witness?

Can I get a witness?

Now ask them

Do you know your name?

They say

Yes, I know my name

For they, these children, have found *them*-

these tablets of despair, vision, overcoming, and

They are telling the stories, while

the folks trying to stop them

But they know that there are realities
darker than death yet
they now know that these stories can pour the truth
and light the consequences
These stories can restore stripped or lost memory
These can stories tell us
Where we are from
When we came from
How we came from
What we can do

These stories, star-birthed
Ready shields
Weapons of gods
Preparing for activation
can set us all free
And you can bet, this time

They won't forget!

When I feel the ancestors stirring, and I don't even know their names

the day after Joy Harjo came to town

separated from this common life by ancient physical deaths

I envision them stepping through portals, strong and brown

Fierce…gentle…free

resolved to find me

my oldest connections to this broken land

their individual names lost from lips for years

lost to me

profound absence of sacred sites that bare feet and sole skins trod

from generation to generation   lost to me

but my ancestors are still dancing   and I don't even know their names

their names stripped from my tongue and thrown into the chasms of greed and fear and mockery and time

others insisted that my lines forget them and bury their voices they moved them place to place

trailing tears as they went out from all they knew

my ancestors are stirring and I don't even know their names

many bodies on battlefields
many bodies as battlefields

…and I don't even know their names

these, my people, hunkered down   this I know
mixed their medicines   this I know
lost and found love   this I know
seeded me in their bellies   this I know
passed shrouded unnamed stories   practices   this I know
left hints in my blood   this I know
died to some old ways to live in new nights/days   this I know

today they swirl above my head
calling me
imploring me to look up
know their presence
feel their ancient names

the others

they say the Croatan are gone

they say the Tuscarora left this land   marched away

they say the Machapunga assimilated

they say a great many truths

they say a great many lies

yet, I am here, holding on to blood-traces mitochondrial DNA autosomal mysteries

words of great grandfathers/mothers

ancestors

whispering through generations

they who are stirring above my head

encircling me

I hear them

I claim them

I write them

They are stirring in me

Beside many others

I don't even know their names

AfroCarolina Black: There is More Than One Way

In case you haven't noticed...
I am Black
Carolina Black
Afro Carolina Black
Afro North Kakalak Black
Eastern Afro Carolina Black
Born of the colonized
The enslaved
The freed
And every possibility between Black
Born down through generations Black
I'm Collard Green, Black
Collard Green and Cornbread Black
Henpecked Salad and Dumplings Black
Fat Back, Salted Streak o' Fat Black
Streak o' lean Black
Not quite like those before me
Nor some after who were/who are
Chitterlings, Black (that ain't me)
See, there is more than one way to be Black
I am watch the Monitors at Sunday in the Park Black
I am Vinegar Barbeque Black
I am 70's and 80's bussed across town Black
I am go to college Black

I am know my history Black
I am know your history Black
I am black enough to know
That while I'm not all Black
That I am enough Black to
Still be treated Black
Whatever that means Black
AfroCarolina Black
I am tobacco warehouse school field trip
Black
I am Vacation Sunday School, Butter Cookies,
Hotdogs on Friday Black
I am Easter Recitation Black
I am teach your Black Children how
to perform that Easter Recitation Black
I am teach your children how to sing Black
Like my mama, my auntie, my grandma Black
My children can sing Black
Sing Black
Sing Black
Three whole note sing Black
I am "that song will save you" Black
I am moved by Church Mother, Joanna Tyson, Black
Reciting Dunbar from her wheelchair Black
Caressing my Black soul Black
I am the witness Black

of life, death, and beyond Black
I am a Petey Pablo Groove Black
Swinging shirts like Helicopters Black
I am march down 5th street in the Eppes High Reunion Parade
Black
with our Maestro Johnny Wooten leading the way, Black
I am "my mama told me stories" Black
I am "my mama gave me hope" Black
I am "my mama taught me not to give a doggone" Black
I am "my mama soothed my soul" Black
I am see my aunties, uncles, cousins all come back from the North, Black
Load up their cars with meal, sausage, and vegetables Black
I am my mama taught me how to care about it all Black
I am my mama taught me when to make that choice Black
I am from a mama who had a mama that shared the stories, too
But also left enough for me to find, Black
I am know who my cousins are" Black
I am "I know who your cousins" are Black
I am a go to the Pow Wow Black
I am a they took our land, Black
The land they did not want to begin with, Black
Now they value our land more than our souls and skins, Black
Want to stomp over the graves my people are buried in, Black
I am waiting for justice to whirl in, Black
I am Afro Carolina Creole Black
Afro Euro Indigenous Black

Black enough to be Black

Black enough to know why

I'm not all Black

Black enough to count it in my making

Of what I love, of what I see, of all my pain

Of all my joy…

I am more Black

I am I hear the drums Black

The ones that call me back Black

I am "I hear the music" Black

Maceo Parker, Billy Taylor, Nina Simone, Roberta Flack

and more and more

Black

I am a daughter of the water, a daughter of the fields, a daughter of the voices

That have taught me to dream beyond Black

I am beyond Black

I am Afro Carolina

In all the ways that matter the most

Way Back Black in These Carolinas

In these Carolinas, there were way-stations
and folks who made ways, and people
who would help Black folk move
so that they could control their own skins
move their own limbs
Live free
Some Maroons down from Dismal,
circling like ghost riders ringing all 'round
would risk their own lives
working the treacherous night in sundown towns
Some like Billy James[3], Black and still rebelling, with
a fee on his head, a government-priced crown
...and that ol' buckra could not stop him
despite what law wanted it to be

"We strong stock and fierce hearts"
wanting to *own* our *own* selves, land *and* sea

See, this Dismal Swamp was really not so dismal
    in this land that kept on stealing liberties

---

3 Smith, William. "Maroons. 2006. https://www.ncpedia.org/maroons

Retrograde

A sister-friend came to me today saying that she felt "off kilter,"
like the world was playing tricks- car wrecked, insurance not covering
all of what she wanted, what she needed for it to cover, having paid
consistently, faithfully, over these years. I told her, as we have
the same number of birthdays, mine before hers, that

"55 is a time! It's a whole mess, Honey!"

we laughed

Then, I told her that it is surely "Mercury in retrograde"

and we laughed some more

Then yielding to our indoctrination…

"Naw, Girl!"

doubling over
steeped in religiosity
having been brought up in "The Word"

I sometimes forget that so much of the God of our Ancients is wrapped in stars

and winds and cleansing water and purging fires in the least rigid of ways, talking, moving earth and skies, rescuing even when we forget the promised power. We revert to westernized boxes of place destiny

fixed time

But God has the world in God's hands, power flowing to and through

Of course, she then reminded me of the time that we had our brooms balanced upright in the middle

of our kitchen floors, a test of magical prowess. She took hers down before I did…said it "creeped her out." It was a joke, and I loved to take them (jokes) far, but in truth, this monument of my inherent power somehow made me feel more able… more free. It stayed…a long time

It was not removed before I said it could be. Nobody dared.

Its ever-standing presence lifted me, emboldened me, and reminded me

that there really was something in me…

Maybe like a too often smothered power

Science, magic, Black girls

God

DeEvolution: Class

Consider…
This ground
These skies
The mighty rolling waters
The small quiet streams
The towering trees
The lowly underbrush

Imagine…
What they have seen
What they have heard
What they have felt
Upon despair descending
Tensing in terror
Drowning in disbelief
Raising the alarm
Splintering earth
while whirling winds
Call the air as witness

Wonder…
How have we come to this?
What have we done to us?
To others?
Negating the wholeness
The many parts of our stories
Our truths

Remember…
The dismemberment
one from another
Removing and reordering
what was never meant to be
& never willing to know
that we, all of us,
were *All* shaped
in the beginning
from formless, colorless, borderless

mouthless breath
born down through time

Children of energy and grace
Crowned in flesh
Once glorious grass

Now...
Segmented
Useless
Murderous
Class

From Shores to This

My people–some crossed wide waters
touched shores, sought and claimed *destiny*
My people–some sea-bound stolen cargo,
triangulated the ways they could be *free*
My people–some walked this patch of earth first,
living and dying here
Rooted in this soil, some hunkered down
Others salted exit trails with tears
My people–all have etched many traumas
and stored them in collective memory
Yet, pieces of generational love
made and birthed their way to *me*

So much told and so much seen
in these witness lands and waterways
that these stories still live and find their homes
in clay lips and whispers steeped in DNA

Windsor of the Water

The Truth and Speculation of Windsor Wade

Sea misted brown skin
skirted the winds and battled the waves
that he might see a glorious
future despite his inglorious condition
...that his conscription to pulling nets
would not be for naught
thinking beyond bondage and living beyond
shackles...He would see Shackleford Banks and Jack's
Lump as victory for himself......for his family

...and so from Windsor to Nancy to
Rachael to others to me...
We still sing the victory!

Ancestral voices still trill in the wind
as today, the wild horses run unfettered, free

Harlowe

Lapping the banks of Clubfoot Creek/The water
whispered tales of witness/Tales of glory days–/Land
tilled by skilled brown hands/ Lush harvests of plenty/Children
of the shores/ waxing strong/muscled in strength/intellect/ & many having
been born free/ fought for "freedom for all"/ The water whispered tales
of witness/Tales of gory days–/Hope bludgeoned & bloodied/Land grabbed
by covetous hands/Kinsmen disappeared into the night/Despair &
Mourning became familiar friends/The creek still whispers/ Tales of
before, now, & to come–/ Tales of tears, resilience, pride, fight, love…

Love Ghosts

Swooshing through thick groves/deep forests/they
ride unseen on currents of urgency/ carrying
messages/ They have seen & they know/that "trouble
will often trouble," but..." joy will return"/ They whisper
"you will regain all worth regaining" /& they sing "weeping
may endure for a night, but joy will come" /& they shed
ghostly tears of commiseration /& drop tender kisses of love
on upturned faces/of these their people/ of these lands/ among
them fly a great granduncle like a grandfather /who shared a still with
the sheriff/ a grandmother who stiffened herself from the
blows of a man drowning in drink/ a fierce protector/ the sweetest
soul/ a Great Auntie who covered in protection all she loved (especially me)/
Ancestors Absalom & Issac who fought in victory/
looking for ways to be even more free/& all/Gratitude
to all these"Love Ghosts"/standing on the banks/ on
the waters/in the fields/ above the trees

Brown Girls Jumping

While seeing The Original Pinettes at Bullets NightClub, New Orleans, Louisiana

I went to Louisiana
Me, a North Carolina Bama
& I found my power
in my hair
the hair that I shook
to an all-girl brass band
Yeah...the baddest
The trumpets blared &
the tuba thumped &
the Brown girls jumped
& shook that hair &
didn't care
if they had a little
a lot
or none
...didn't care
If it was grown
bought
or won by trial
...didn't care
what vile people said
Their manes were present
or invisibly gifted through
special dispensation from God
An aura just
flowing
around their shoulders
down their back
swinging
blowing
showing the world that
it doesn't matter what the people say
Their strength comes from some

ethereal

divine
supernatural
sublime force
cloaked in music &
revealed as a spirit
felt behind
closed eyes
tingling in
dancing feet &
snapping fingers
The train from their manes
envelops
endows
entreats
favor and power
See, if Delilah had really felt her own
She would have left Sampson alone
For his emasculation did not lead to her divination
Swing your hair, Brown girls &
cast your cares
to that which protects & inspires
your own strength
Brown girls jumping
Music thumping in NOLA
Me, a NC Bama on a holiday mission...
Taking two fish, a few loaves
a little hot sauce...
Hands folded in prayer...
...praying that this holy meal multiplies
before my season ends

AfroCarolina Land, Sea, & Stew

We are land, sprawling soul, & skin
steeped in Carolina sand & soil
It has built us in the best of times
covered us in the worst
Our hearts beat telltale notes, we are
of this place, these banks–outer, inner, & beyond
We are water, fluid & flowing, shimmering…
sometimes rising as waves of knowing
showing the world that our depth is more
than deep; it is complex-water wailing, water
washing, water witnessing, singing through sounds
The sea, a birth canal that his spit us upon the shores
reminded us to breathe, to cry, but not to die
We are these– fed holy fish, tomato broth, bacon,
potatoes, asked by earth & ocean to trust, to believe,
to be made whole, misted & sanctified by the voices
of our people, this sand, & the tides that rock in & out

To: **Whom It May Concern**
RE: **Black Joy**
Upon the purchase of a Black History Month t-shirt
one that almost shut me down in my local Target
chanting at me from the racks
Radiate Black Joy
I determined that it was my time to shine, radiate, unwind
ALL of my joy! Yet

as I lay the shirt across my bed, face
set on 'grateful' for my find, my ancestors moved
from my belly, up into my opened ears, and I heard their whispers
words not relegated to the intentional, traditional observations of
Black History. I stood, picked up the shirt, slid it over my head, and
was divinely compelled to consider, to list the layers, for myself and
others, of what it means to radiate Black joy. For if we are honest, this
Black joy, as a construct, is shaped by the misshapen circumstances of
history, for indeed Black joy is

what is birthed between bouts of Black pain
It is molded to sustain
It is compelled to keep moving
through one degree of uncertainty to the next
It is the production of delicacies
from disposable waste
It is the retention of The Spirit
that has been carried in ancestors
from generation to generation
hidden and released in clearings
introduced through uttered prayers and praise, and
It emerges in various forms
sometimes like tears

sometimes like immovability
It can even hide under other feelings
mask in mysteries,
cloak in glances, in ways of speaking
laugh behind closed eyes and lips
While yet another layer of joy plants the seeds of the knowledge
that there are golden pieces of Black gifting, of Black strength, even of Black
prophecy that cannot be removed from Black existence.
That is that Black joy-
knowing that even in derision, there is provision
in this joy that secrets us
and the gifts that save us
This joy that reminds us that
trouble don't last always
weeping endures for a night
joy comes in the morning light

And at times, good times, Black joy requires Black
bodies to throw back their heads and
laugh loudly and move freely
play Spades
The Dozens
dance
love
create
create
create
share
care
Save the whole world

The children know that there is love
Just there
In Black joy
And for ALL who may be concerned
Know this-
While this joy is juxtaposed to pain
the glory is that it can
Emerge
again, and again
Black Joy
Shine
Radiate
Refine
Create
More and more
Great God! Black joy!
You tell anyone else who wants to know
Just tell them to go on and
know that there is more in store
from this brilliant, unbelievably resilient
Black
Joy

Hallowed Grounds: Sacred Sites of African American Memory

In my mind, there are sacred sites…
Striding and struggling
Striations of strain and strength...
In memories I once lived and those I inherited
I marvel at how they and I "made it over" as if I floated in on the broken but braced backs of a superhuman ancestral brood
Perhaps fire-baptized for a time such as this
For how on earth, Heaven, or hell…
Dare I move clay lips to laugh, lie, cry, love, preen, protest, speak and write life, and dodge death?
Lord, I realize…
These sanctified places of terror, trial, and triumph are ordered in my thoughts, a reminder that true freedom is always bought with a price of great sacrifice and justified only through an ointment of redemption
So, the Spirit moved…
among these places
Buried a flaming message in my forebears, even while they were moaning in manacles
Hallowed be thy name
Inspired their holy dance while in deprivation
Hallowed be thy name
Anticipated the Gilded Grace that would carry them
Hallowed be thy name
Praised The Divine for answered prayers whispered only in their thoughts
Hallowed be thy name
In this lowly, fickle, land
Hallowed, hallowed, hallowed…
be thy name

The Air Bears Witness

Air

Shaped breath of Divinity

Fuel of humanity

A silent sentient ambassador

Indeed

Utterance

Mobility

Laughter

Love

All require...

Air

Ever present

Sustainer of life

Respect due

Respect due

And yet on these todays

Yea, even from the beginnings of days

Air bears ugly witness

To the first whispers of dishonored death

Death signaled by

Raised brows

Tears
Anger
Fears
Agitated spirits
That tell darkened depraved minds
That there is indeed no other way
Air stares soundlessly
As thoughts break through cracked lips
Words traveling on its currents
Into ears of waiting co-conspirators
Or simply float
Then sink back into skin
To settle and harden in the minds that conceived it
And the hearts that believe that Breath Disrupted
Is the only way
To take control of these uncertain times
Air is obliged
To be pulled in and out of lungs
Irrespective
Of the evil
Of the good
Air is there shifting uneasily
When the brute punches straight through her face and breaks her teeth
Blood pouring from the spaces
Underneath, indiscreet
Air is there wildly uncomfortable
When insanity, profanity, corruption, brutality
Meet in alleyways and leave mothers
Planning and digging graves
Air is there when the clamoring mob says

"Let's catch one unaware"
And Air conspires with Fire and watches as they bring the rope
and tie it tightly on wearied feet that have tried to run
Dragging life down dark roads
In pop-up sundown towns
Air sees tracks of blood relentlessly
Circle this place
From age to age
Circle this place
Air sees it all
Trapped in even
The most unholy
The most undignified
Rooms
Makeshift tombs

While Bright Air's charge is to sustain
The flesh in this domain
Man's refrains
Of violence and misery
Savagely redirect its mission
And Air remains
To give testimony
Eternal testimony
For Air is divinely compelled
Righteously compelled
To stoically bear witness
To it all

Stars and Sin

Looking at stars is sin?
I am born in sin
I'm looking at stars to find myself
To find my way
To find an answer
To find the voice in the stars

Many of the righteous
Followed stars
Found Jesus
following stars
What a journey!
Looking at stars
to find their way
to hear That Voice
to see It clear

Mama Harriet looked at stars
Mama Harriet knew God
The God she knew…
you think that god is
your god, too?
Sounds good to say it
but Her God
was in the night air
and in her mind
and in those stars

Have you looked at
what happens
when you look at stars?
Looking at stars has
slowed death
Looking at stars has
saved lives
Not looking, though
sometimes meant not living

Telling me not to look at stars
Telling me not to live
Telling me to lower my eyes
Telling me to hear your Jesus
Is my Jesus your Jesus?
My Jesus was born
under the stars
Ain't no sin in him

My Jesus was born under stars
Ancient books say that his star
shone brightly above him
Folks have walked for years
guided by the stars
But now messages from the stars
are devilish?

Stars worship God
even better than flesh
Line up and listen
better than flesh

I look at stars
That makes me sin?

I look at stars
because I am born in sin
I look at stars
They are messengers
of Science and Salvation
because they know God

And I want God
to show me the way
And I want God
to keep me

Black Is A Well: Multiverse Interlude

Many times/I sit high on the hilltop/ as the Sun begins its descent/beyond the Sea/ and in the times that this glowing orb/ has escaped my view/ I've considered the whys of the world/ for as far as we have gone/ we've not gone far enough/ The hate seems to never stop its flaring/ I think this as sure/as the rising and falling of days/ days that seem stuck on sameness/ too often bittered by the sadness of a moaning earth/ *Will we ever reach enough?/ Will it ever be enough/* and then as sure as the day leaves/ Night stars begin piercing and pen lighting the Sky/ Tides roll in and out/ and Universe's sultried refrain/ melts my moments of fear/ and brings me back to life/still sitting/high on the hilltop/ waiting for more to come/ I still myself for the cosmos to whisper/ to sing/ to run hope notes like Rivers/ dancing in my head / to pouring like Jacob's well/ straight down into my soul/*living water*/lighting it on fire/whispers to flames

Black is a well
A sanctuary of solace
A space for refueling
Pouring buckets of relief
Like Living Water rained down

Rained down in ancient days....

Black is a well
whose life extends
Extends from the Holy Shores
and stretches down like a track running

Running to find a blanket like Home

Black is a well
A reservoir full of rheumatic hands
Hands that stitched together quilts
Quilts of reflection and direction
Direction that points to a new home

Black is a well
A well whispering The Way
A Way paved around and beyond
Following Moonbeams and Stars

Stars singing in the pause of Heaviness and Hope

Hope that floats like Whispers from the Multiverse

welling and swelling

    in the endless Night Air

        again and again

About the Author

Regina YC Garcia is a poet, language artist, and English professor. She is a graduate of The University of North Carolina at Chapel Hill where she earned a BA in Speech Communication with a Concentration in the Oral Interpretation of Literature. She additionally earned an MA in Adult Education from East Carolina University, as well as a Graduate Certificate in Multicultural and Transnational Literature. She currently teaches English and is the Coordinator of Global Programs at Pitt Community College.

Garcia's literary work primarily centers around issues related to family and culture, social justice, and human rights. She is committed to effecting change through the persistent literary address of inequities, inequalities, and disparities. She is also committed to the uplift of consciousness and spirit through education and the arts.

She is the 2021 NSDAR American Heritage Poetry Award Winner, and in 2025 she was awarded the NSDAR American Heritage Woman in the Arts. Additionally, Garcia is a 2024 NCLR James Applewhite Finalist, a 2024 Jaki Shelton Green Finalist and a 2023 and 2024 Pushcart Nominee. Her publications of poetry and video poetry can be found in a variety of journals and anthologies including the *South Florida Poetry Journal*, *Up the Staircase Quarterly*, The Book of Black, *Kakalak*, *I Tried Not to Write*, *Main Street Rag*, *The Amistad*, Tulane University's *Sacred 9 Project*, *The AutoEthnographer*, *Fiyah* and numerous others. Her narration and poetry have also been featured (in *The Black Light Project*, a documentary which was the subject of an Emmy Award winning episode of PBS *Muse: An Art Show*.

Garcia's first short collection of poetry, *The Firetalker's Daughter*, was released by Finishing Line Press in March 2023. *Whispers from the Multiverse* marks her first full-length collection of poetry.

www.ingramcontent.com/pod-product-compliance
Lightning Source LLC
Chambersburg PA
CBHW020534120726
47904CB00003B/1064
9780985287733